IMPERFECT BEING

My journey of self-discovery

Stephen Ochieng

Scripture quotations are taken from the Holy Bible, New Revised Standard Version Bible: Anglicized Edition, copyright 1989, 1995, Division of Christian Education of the National Council of the Churches of Christ in the United States of America. Used by permission. All rights reserved."

Visit my website at www.ochiengfamily.wordpress.com
Printed in the United States of America

First Printing: 2020

ISBN-13-978-0-578-74448-3

Dedication

I dedicate this book to my mother, Joyce Ochieng, who showed me what it truly means to live like Christ not just in words but by actions. To my lovely wife Rachel who pushed me to get this published "by any means necessary". To my lovely daughter Aisosa who put her artistic touch to design a beautiful cover page.

To my sister Rachel and brother in-law Chris for supporting me and loving me unconditionally. I consider it a privilege to have taken care of my nephews Amani, Alex, and Anthony because it prepared me to care for my son, Asifiwe.

Table of Contents

Introduction 5

Chapter 1 10

Chapter 2 15

Chapter 3 20

Chapter 4 25

Chapter 5 27

Chapter 6 30

Chapter 7 33

Chapter 8 39

Chapter 9 42

Chapter 10 44

Chapter 11 48

Chapter 12 50

Chapter 13 53

Chapter 14 57

Chapter 15 58

Chapter 16 60

Chapter 17 62

Chapter 18 63

Chapter 19 64

Chapter 20 66

Chapter 21 68

Chapter 22 69

Chapter 23 71

Introduction

People around the world seek to understand their purpose in life. Where did we come from? Why are we here? Is there a bigger role and a higher purpose we have to play? What is that purpose? Is there an all-powerful God? What does His existence or absence mean in our lives? Are we just born to live and die?

These are all valid questions that I've asked myself over and over again and there was always a nagging sense of urgency in my spirit and a deeper yearning for something greater that forced me to delve deeper into who I truly was as a person. A search that was free of any past influences or current circumstances. The things I valued around me suddenly didn't seem all that important.

One summer afternoon as I walked home from the park, I stared up into the deep blue sky and felt a tug in my heart that suggested that surely there had to be more to life than this. I felt I was wandering through life like a castaway in the middle of the sea clinging onto a plank of wood with no hope of rescue. Crisis has a way of bringing a man back to his senses; but in every crisis there is a turning point. As I contemplated my future, I saw before my eyes a distinct vision of a path that I had to take not just very soon, but immediately. I had to act either to avert the looming danger of a purposeless existence or make it worse by doing nothing. These were the distinct words I said to myself that afternoon. "I stand on the edge of a cliff and see a beast running straight toward me. It has its jaws wide open, baring its razor-sharp fangs at me as saliva drips from its blood-stained mouth. Behind me the darkness of the precipice beckons and I'm ignorant of the dangers it holds. I need to make a decision fast. I can't ignore my situation lest I get mauled and eaten alive. If I don't act, I will be torn limb by limb by this ferocious animal that's hell bent on filling its belly and ending my life. I'm going to die either way so without a second thought I twist my body backwards into the air and I jump. Not knowing what awaits me at the bottom. Will the jagged rocks impale me on impact? Or will the icy blast of cold water briefly envelope my entire body and help me forget my fear."

Back to the present. In that brief moment of uncertainty I'm glad I made the jump. A leap of faith that I knew would be rewarded. That there was more to life than just a job, a family, a spouse, a hobby or everything else for that matter. At that stage in my life I was unemployed and hurting from a failed relationship, but these things suddenly paled in comparison to the emptiness in my spirit. My heart yearned for answers to deal with that emptiness. I looked up at the sky once more and imagined myself floating off the ground, soaring higher and higher past the wispy white clouds and stopping thousands of feet in the air to stare down at the world.

I was hoping to catch a glimpse of myself and take my body along but as I surveyed what was before me, the vastness of the oceans and continents, I felt so small and insignificant. I was angry at myself for missing out on missed opportunities and alone in a country that I felt I didn't belong. Yet I understood that many men and women overcame worse odds than mine and have gone on to succeed.

I still had a duty to perform on earth and just because I did not know it yet did not mean I had to give up. All I had to do was keep searching in a book I had overlooked for so long. The Bible.

This is my first book and I wish there was a perfect formula for introducing it. It's a collection of my writing from 2012 to the present and by the time I publish this the world will hopefully be past the COVID-19 pandemic. There was a silver lining in all of this, and it allowed me to do something I put off for so long. No more excuses. Did you use your time at home wisely?

My book is also a collection of my thoughts as I navigated through a difficult period in my life. My pursuit of God often posed more questions than answers, but it challenged me not only to move forward but to take responsibility of the present. I'd like you to look at this also not as a chronological account of events taking place in my life but as purposeful incisive thoughts that allowed me to vent and pray to God in a way that people close to me may not understand. Go ahead. Randomly go to page 50 for instance but RELATE the verse I am discussing there to YOUR OWN LIFE.

God will meet you exactly where you are in your life. We sometimes think we need to clean up our act before approaching God but your imperfection is ironically the best place to be because you can finally look inward and decide whether you want to trust God or keep repeating the same mistakes.

This is a glimpse into my spiritual journey as a single man seeking answers in the Bible when I failed to find them in the world. These are my raw interpretations of scripture and I pray they speak to you as they did to me.

Chapter One

GOD IS CREATOR AND SPIRIT

Genesis 1:1-2

"In the beginning GOD CREATED the heavens and the earth. 2 The earth was without form and void, and darkness was upon the face of the deep; and the SPIRIT of God was moving over the face of the waters."

These two verses answer two important questions. What God can do and who He is. God has the power to CREATE something out of nothing. So, He is the CREATOR of ALL things. I feel like I live in a time when we do not recognize how complex and beautiful the world is and lose sight of the things that make us unique. However, I look at my own life, and refuse to accept that things 'just happen'.

I am holding on to too many things mentally and spiritually and it is time I let go. I'd like to see the creation story as a lesson or example of how to REFRESH ALL aspects of my life. No more looking back. Since NOW is my BEGINNING, God can CREATE something beautiful out of me out of NOTHING. I am a clean slate. I am a foundation laid down preparing for bigger things to happen. I am not tied down to my past failures or insecurities. It does not matter how I feel. What matters is me making the first steps towards recovery and AWAY from the darkness.

Despite the misdirection (FORMLESS) and emptiness (VOID) of the past, despite the lack of vision (DARKNESS) that makes me stumble. the spirit of God still MOVED within me. I must tap into that Spirit because it is what will transform me into a new man.

My Son is changing as well. He is not the helpless boy I once held in my arms. He is just over a year old now and so full of life. He is walking confidently and doing his best to navigate around our small apartment. A few months earlier I was thrilled when he was finally able to sit up by himself and now he expresses himself in so many different ways. There is meaning in his squeals, shouts, and grunts. The look of recognition he gives me when he says "DADA" warms my heart in ways I can't express.

Scripture says we are God's children no matter how old we are and I can see a glimpse of the tenderness God shows us despite our faults. God is so quick to forgive because we are little children. He nurtures us, advises us and guides us into spiritual maturity so that we can stop doing childish things.

My son looks forward to each morning and I must do the same. Nothing is guaranteed and so I must value EVERY MOMENT God gives me. No more excuses, but more importantly no more dwelling on the past. I am a new man.

Genesis 1: 3-4

And God said, "Let there be LIGHT": and there was light. 4 And God saw that the light was good: and God SEPARATED the light from the darkness."

I must speak things into existence and part of my responsibility is to say that I DO NOT WANT DARKNESS IN MY LIFE. Make bold statements not simply as a mantra but a way to make it part of my spiritual fabric. Let light be embedded into your skin like blood flowing through your veins. There is a clear distinction between LIGHT and darkness and the ONLY way to keep darkness out is to introduce the LIGHT. Therefore, focus on the things that bring out the light in you. Leave the things that feel good in the moment yet only leave your heart dark and empty.

So being created by God goes beyond just blindly accepting a set of rules and following what I'm told. It's a more WHOLESOME EXPERIENCE that promotes unity and establishes that we all as human beings came from one place despite our economic background, social up bringing or political affiliation. There is a point in time, thousands or millions of years ago that we can point to and say we all came from this ONE place.

As I continue to read the Bible, there are verses that strengthen this point. However, my goal is to do a step by step analysis of individual verses and deconstruct their current meaning.

Light as a symbol of God

Genesis 1:3-4

And God said, "Let there be LIGHT"; and there was light. And God saw that the light was good; and God separated the light from darkness.

The first thing God created was LIGHT. In a time of complete confusion, emptiness, chaos and darkness, light was the first sign of clarity. The first symbol of illumination not only in the physical world but in the spiritual one as well.

There is a clear distinction between light and darkness. The two do not mix and light will ALWAYS take precedence over darkness. It's not a coincidence that light was the first thing God chose to create. Light was a visual representation and manifestation of who He is in a world without direction.

God is the creator of everything

God is orderly

The main theme in the first chapter of Genesis is CREATION. It shows the power that God possesses to create something out of nothing. Similarly, it's a reflection of God's ORDERLY nature. When God creates, there is a specific routine to how He works and the story of creation shows the care with which He gives every single thing on earth and what role it plays. He creates each thing separately from another and this is evidence of how carefully He works.

Chapter Two

MAN AND ANIMALS

GENESIS 1:26

The purpose of this segment is to identify specific verses in Genesis that give me instructions on how to take care of myself. That means my body, my mind and my spirit. This will range from everything, from how to pray to how to control my emotions. This portion of my writing is about our/my responsibility towards ANIMALS, and **GENESIS 1:26 says "Let us make man in our image, after our likeness; and let them have dominion over all..."** (The living things on this planet/on earth.) Genesis 1:26 says that (or that is) God made ME in his own image and likeness and gave ME the responsibility to be in charge of every single living thing around me. Now, I'm not a vet, zoo keeper or animal expert of any kind to appreciate just how unique, diverse and beautiful other animals are. In fact, it would be slightly harsh to say that all animals simply live to survive otherwise we wouldn't have pets to keep us company.

I have learned a lot just from watching other animals interact and no matter how harsh the environment they live in is or just how hard they fight to survive even when the odds are against them, they keep going on. Their own experiences are similar to ours. A lioness will defend her cubs to the death if she has to. A hen will fight off a hawk or a deadly snake to keep her chicks safe. A school of dolphins will work together to find food or fend off prey. A turkey will...I don't care much about turkeys to be honest. They are the meanest birds I ever met. As wild as Ostriches are, turkeys must be a close second. Brief story...

{When I was growing up in Kisumu, I often went to play at my friend Rafael's house but occasionally we'd prefer to go to his neighbor's house who lived on the opposite side of the street. What I learned the few times I went there was that Turkeys are just as adept as dogs in identifying friend from foe. Rafael's friend would kick the soccer ball right among them and they'd almost apologetically clear the path to let him through as he retrieved the ball.

In my case, or in anyone's case for that matter who didn't belong to that household, those turkeys would glare at you and dare you to do something stupid as soon as you came close to them. They'd strut around, fluff their feathers to make themselves look bigger -as if they weren't gigantic already- and they'd stomp the ground so hard we could hear the audible "Thump!" The few times I was foolish enough to kick the ball in their direction, I'd run in the opposite direction just to be safe. There was also the myth that turkeys would attack anything with bright colors. Why on God's green earth would I wear red or have another color that screamed "I'm here! I'm here! Come get me" every time I went to that house? It was either coincidence or bad luck. Either way, Superman had kryptonite to deal with and I had turkeys to contend with in my childhood.} Story time over...

But I digress. It's no coincidence that human beings are on top of the food chain. God gave us animals not just as pets, but as food to nourish our bodies. (God bless you vegetarians and vegans!)

Now obviously with that power comes enormous responsibility as well. As much as I despised snakes and couldn't stand them I came to find out that some of the venom extracted from them isn't just used to make anti venom, but is used in drugs that help reduce blood pressure in human beings. My mother and many members on her side of the family have had a history of high blood pressure and I can recall one particular incident when my mother was so sick she had to be admitted to a hospital. It's the only time I saw one of my sisters in tears and only now do I realize the severity of my mother's condition.

Does it mean I will sit calmly as a snake slithers by? Absolutely not. But the truth is I have a greater appreciation of what animals of every kind can do. Even the ones that we think aren't useful at all. God didn't tell us to hurt them or mistreat them for our pleasure, but to be in charge of them in a way that when necessary, is mutually beneficial.

And just a side note. I miss my dog Terror. When he died, I think it was one of the first times that I genuinely prayed to God not only to comfort me but to see him again when I went to heaven. It was a sad night when he died I cried myself to sleep. My sister, Dory had spent weeks cleaning up the tumor on his leg and dressing it with bandages when the blood seeped through it. Watching something you love suffer is heartbreaking and I wouldn't wish it on anyone on this planet. People who don't own dogs or haven't had them long enough to grow attached to them wouldn't really understand but our dog Terror was special. (That's twice now I've shed a tear. Thinking about how much I miss my dad and how much I miss my dog. Steve you're going soft but its ok. I'm only human and I thank God for all my experiences as I grow into a more mature Christian man.)

Chapter Three

SEX/UNDERSTANDING SEXUALITY

Genesis 1:27

Sex is a touchy subject for me and even to this day I struggle with understanding my sexuality. It's not because I feel awkward talking about it but I think it's because it's brought me more pain than joy and it's a feeling that has lingered over the years. Traumatic is probably too strong of a word to describe it.

As a single man, am I attracted to a woman because I care about her or is it because I want to sleep with her? I've realized that there is a fine line between lust and genuine attraction. I understand that it is normal for the body to react to what the mind sees but I must practice self-control. I don't do it to suppress any sexual urge and neither do I do it to feel pure about myself. These are secondary reasons that oversimplify the issue. I am doing it to honor God and this is why.

I'm happy about how I handled my last relationship with.....Writing her name down will only stir up memories but I can confidently say that I wanted to get to know her for who she was and I wanted to open up my heart to her in a way I hadn't done in the past. In the process, she accepted me for who I was. The good and the bad, and she shared her secrets as well that made me realize there is real hope in finding love. In the end it just didn't work out and accepting it was the hardest part. We were at a party and she pulled me aside to the kitchen and said those words no one in love wants to hear. "Steve, you're a great guy but…."

I'm still single and I don't think it's for lack of trying, it's just that at this point in my life, and women really aren't a priority. I constantly need to ask myself this question every single time I get close to someone. "Am I with her for the right reasons?"

The bible is pretty clear about the sanctity of sex WITHIN a marriage and I frankly don't have any excuses for NOT doing the right thing.

Genesis 1:27, says that, "God created man in his own image and said to them, 'Be fruitful and multiply and fill the earth and subdue it."

God created US in his own image. He created ME in his own image; therefore he UNDERSTANDS how I feel. He didn't create me without feelings and neither did he create me to do nothing. God gave us the mandate or power to have sex, WITHIN a marriage. So if there is anyone who's an expert on sex then it must be God. As I continue to study the word I pray I will get to understand and appreciate my sexuality.

My prayer to you right now Lord is to help me understand my feelings when it comes to sex and attraction. Give me the words and courage to speak to a woman I care about in a loving way, in a gentle way that will conform to your wisdom on Jesus, Love, and Marriage. Amen.

God gave me LIFE. Genesis 2:7 "Then the Lord God formed man of dust from the ground, and breathed into his nostrils the breath of LIFE; and man became a living being."

I have a very intimate relationship with God. He is a part of me as much as I am a part of him. My existence isn't some random biological occurrence but a deliberate step by God to show that my life matters. The same love that God has shown me is the same love I must show others regardless of what they have done to me. God requires obedience. (The Garden of Eden as a metaphor for my life/ talents. Just as God made Adam and Eve responsible for the garden, God has given me the responsibility to look after my life (My body, mind spirit) Otherwise there are consequences to not doing it.

God has given me specific gifts that I must nurture. It was man's responsibility to take care of the Garden of Eden and God told him he may eat of any and every tree in the garden except the tree of knowledge of good and evil and the day he shall eat of it he will die. God requires OBEDIENCE, and we often do not know or realize the consequences of our actions unless we OBEY him.

God is a REMINDER

Last weekend I forgot to return my library book. Unfortunately, the library that I borrowed the book from is at least 30 minutes away. I intended to give the book to my brother in law who visited me briefly this morning to return it, but I completely forgot to give it to him. The fine isn't hefty by any means, but I couldn't help but chastise myself for my forgetfulness.

When God instructed Abraham to leave his father's country, He PROMISED to bless him and future generations in a land that Abraham never even knew. By FAITH, Abraham left the place of his birth and followed God's PROMISE. Over the course of their relationship, God often REMINDED Abraham of the initial PROMISE He made to him. He REMINDED Abraham that not only would his descendants rival the number of stars in the sky, but that Abraham would have a son born of his wife Sarah. Now Sarah and Abraham were both too old to have children but, in the bible,, God had a habit of specializing in the impossible.

That's the God I serve. My God will REMIND me of his promise to protect me in a foreign land. My God will REMIND me of the hope that he has given me and keep me focused on following his WILL for my life. Like most Christians I face challenges that seem difficult to overcome but I take HOPE and develop COURAGE in the fact that even though I may forget sometimes, God REMINDS me of the PROMISE He made to me of a better future.

Once God has established or said something that he WILL do, it's not just his duty to EXECUTE that plan but it's in his very NATURE to REMIND me of the PROMISE that He made.

Chapter Four

EMPLOYMENT/DEALING WITH UNEMPLOYMENT

The life of an unemployed man is hard. I might be stating the obvious to most people but to some who haven't gone through it; it's the most challenging part of growing up and becoming an adult. I didn't have a wife and children to take care of then and neither was I homeless. Both things of which I am eternally grateful to God for avoiding at that time, and yet, the pressure and the mental strength to keep moving became physically and emotionally draining. I felt alone, worthless and really unable to focus on what specific job I really wanted. At that stage, I prayed for a job, ANY job. I was unemployed for so long I didn't think I was worthy of even getting an office job. All I could think of was manual labor or a minimum wage job. I'm not proud of the hardship I went through and I'm not saying this to gain any sympathy. Like one of my high school teachers used to say, "A man who makes his own bed lies in it." I took responsibility for my actions and endured them as best as I could but nothing took away the pain. I wanted a job, not just to gain my sanity back, not just to get money but I honestly wanted a job to feel I was worth something. That I mattered in the world and that I could contribute in some way to help everyone around me.

There are moments in a man's life where you experience the lowest of the low and unemployment can have a serious impact on his self-esteem.

Chapter Five

DECISIONS; MORE THAN MEET THE EYES

Genesis 13:10-11

When Lot made the decision to separate himself and his family from Abram, he chose to go to Sodom. On the surface, Sodom looked like the perfect place to settle down. At the time it was probably as close as you could come to a bustling modern-day city that was full of traders, businessmen and entertainment of all kinds. He was probably tired of living a nomadic life and deep down in his heart wanted a more sedentary lifestyle. Moving to Sodom would give him a chance to be his own man and make decisions for himself without having to worry about the watchful eye of his uncle Abram. The separation would give him freedom that he craved and the independence would let him experience the world more.

Just like Lot, we've made rash decisions that at first appear logical but in the long run prove to be regrettable. Just because something looks good doesn't mean it's a worthwhile investment in the long run. Lot made an emotional decision based on what he saw and how he felt rather than taking his time to make a smarter decision. He had likely made up his mind long before the meeting with Abram and had his eye on the valley all along.

Genesis 13:10-11 says that **"Lot lifted up his eyes, and saw that the Jordan Valley was well watered everywhere like the garden of the Lord, like the land of Egypt, in the direction of Zoar... so Lot chose for himself all the Jordan Valley journeyed east."**

Verse 13 of the same chapter sheds more light on the type of city and people Lot was getting himself into. They were **"wicked and great sinners of the Lord."**

Not only was Sodom a corrupt place but it was politically unstable as well. Kings who were former allies rebelled against each other and the ones who were defeated died horrible deaths by falling into bitumen pits. Lot's intentions to move to Sodom were noble, and it would be harsh to blame him for settling among these people. It's important to note that every story in the bible, however tragic, is a lesson on how to make better decisions in our own lives. God always provides a way out and even though Lot and his family were captured in the midst of war, Abram did not hesitate to rescue him. Whatever mistakes he had made in the past were inconsequential (wow. I should have said irrelevant, but I like the word inconsequential. What a mouthful) and his uncle, Abram, through God's help, was there when he needed him the most.

Chapter Six

God is my PROTECTOR my COMFORTER

Genesis 15:1
"FEAR NOT Abram, I am your shield; your reward shall be great."

God is my comforter, my protector, my assurance in times of uncertainty, doubt, fear or hopelessness. He GUARANTEES that under His protection I will be rewarded for my faith in Him. Just like Abraham at the time, my future is uncertain, yet I must NOT be afraid because God is with me, and He WILL reward me. Abraham was concerned that he was never going to have a child and that his heir would be Eliezer of Damascus, born of a slave. God assured him that he would indeed have his own son and that his descendants would be as countless as the stars in the night sky. Verse 6 goes on to say that Abraham **"BELIEVED the Lord; and he reckoned to him as RIGHTEOUSNESS."**

Abraham the FOREIGNER

Not only did God tell Abraham to go to a foreign land and He would make him successful there, but He also promised that his descendants would endure incredible hardship for a greater purpose. **Genesis 15:13 "Know of a surety that your descendants will be sojourners in a land that is not theirs, and will be slaves there, and they will be oppressed for four hundred years."** I am an immigrant in the United States. The word immigrant seems to have taken various meanings over recent years and most of them negative yet just like Abraham I am a man living far away from home. I miss my family every day, I wish I had my closest friends with me yet I know I made the right decision to move here. There was a greater purpose to my journey, and I have to make it worthwhile no matter what it takes.

There is nothing unique about my story because I follow in the footsteps of many who set out for a better life. I've been insulted; I've been called a criminal, but despite all this I am exactly where God wants me to be.

God rewards faithfulness

Genesis 17:1-2 "I am God Almighty walk before me and be blameless. And I will make my covenant between me and you, and will multiply you exceedingly. "

Another fundamental principle about God is that he rewards faithfulness. God loved Abraham deeply and wanted to give him everything that he promised him. If I walk before God blameless, that means I have no guilt about my life, past or present. I have no fear about the decisions I make and I have the COURAGE to pursue dreams and goals of my choice. The covenant/promise between God and I is established and can never be broken. It is guaranteed. However, it is up to me to open my heart and be receptive to God's word which will then teach me to walk before God, blameless.

Chapter Seven

FRUSTRATION AND DECISIONS

Genesis Chapter 16

Frustration, anger and disappointment often lead to impulsive or rash decisions. The frustration can range from being disrespected by a friend or being abandoned by your family. Similarly, it can also come from falling short of your goals despite giving it your best. Obviously every situation varies and for some people it stings more than usual but the prevailing hurtful feeling is the same regardless of the circumstance. Some people may even casually shrug their shoulders at your problem and tell you to "man up" or say it's "just part of life" but that never magically makes the pain go away.

Whatever disappointments we've had to endure in life, it's normal to feel defeated and alone in those moments. It's better to feel something rather than being completely apathetic to the situation.

Before Sarah there was Sarai.

In Genesis Chapter 16, I imagine Abram's wife Sarai, sitting alone by a fire, watching the flames dancing feverishly beside a hearth. She's so close she could touch it yet she still feels cold. She wraps her shawl tightly across her shoulders and nuzzles her chin to her chest to feel warmer. Sarai waits for her husband Abram to arrive but secretly wishes it shouldn't have to be like this every night. She loves him dearly and knows he'd do anything for her but it pains her that she doesn't have a child to keep her company. Her Egyptian maid Hagar walks into the room to say something to Sarai but she can tell she's too nervous to speak.

"The poor girl is afraid I'll lash out at her again," Sarai says to herself. So, she just continues staring at the fire until the girl leaves. The burning wood crackles softly when an ember shoots out and lands beside Sarai. It glows briefly like a twinkling star but dies out seconds later. It's then that an idea comes to Sarai. She contemplates it in her head and wonders what her husband would think. "If he loves me he'll do it," she whispers. "Besides, I'm not as young as I once was so what do I have to lose. He did mention to me that God will provide an heir so this must be it. This must be a sign." The more Sarai thinks about it, the more she's convinced that this is what God wants her to do. Somewhat refreshed, she takes off her shawl, folds it up and places it gently beside her. She gets up slowly off the ground, her muscles screaming at her as she steadies herself. She's tempted to call Hagar for help but quickly changes her mind.

"This has to be it. Surely it has to be it," she says tentatively trying to make herself believe her own words. She picks up a small bowl on the table and scoops up some water from her clay pot. After years and years of praying and after years and years of disappointment it felt good to be alive again. It felt even better to be decisive and not wait anymore.

Each sip of water that Sarai takes from the bowl clears her mind and gives her courage. She puts it down, exits the tent and is surprised by how dark it is outside. The gentle breeze from the east feels good on her skin. She closes her eyes, lifts her head up and takes a deep breath. The faint smell of roasted meat and freshly cut wood fills her nostrils.

"You know you shouldn't be out here this late," a voice says to her from the darkness. "You'll get sick again."

It was her husband Abram. Sarai was slightly startled but didn't flinch. She was a child of the desert and nothing surprised her anymore. She knew he meant well but ignored him. Her eyes had adjusted to the darkness as the half-moon peered over the clouds.

Her silence was all Abram needed to know that she had something important to say. That's what years of marriage had taught him. Their silent communication spoke more than any words that passed between them and it made him love her even more. This was it, Sarai thought. This was the moment she'd been planning for but she could hardly open her lips. All the things she wanted to carefully explain to him faded away from her mind like a mist so she blurted out the first clear thought that came to her. "The girl."

Her husband put his arms across his chest wondering what she meant. She heard him breathing and could tell he was uneasy. He cut the silence and replied, "What about her?"

"She...she." Sarai knew she had to say it but why was her throat suddenly so dry and her tongue so heavy? "The girl can give you a child. She can give you the son you've longed for. It's the only way out of this," Sarai said quickly. Abram had also learned not to upset his wife when she'd made up her mind about something, and this was one of those times. "It's our way out of what?" He asked. "You know I love you and God said..." Sarai finally turned around to face him. "God said I was going to have a child, and this is the only way how. Look at me Abram, I'm old. I can barely walk as it is and I'm tired. I'm..."

Sarai let her words trail off, quietly hoping that he would understand her anguish. She rarely let her emotion show but there was no one she would have rather talked to than Abram. He let out a deep sigh, cleared his throat and contemplated what to say. "Maybe we can wait just a little longer. Just a few more days, maybe weeks but it will happen. I know it will."

Sarai moved closer to him and saw a small streak of moonlight reflecting off his eyes. "Maybe I won't be alive while you wait. Have you thought about that?" She said curtly. With that, she abruptly brushed past him and went back to the tent while wrapping her shoal tighter over her body. She knew the chill she suddenly felt wasn't from the cold desert air. Even though she wanted to sit by the fire again for warmth she knew it was a waste of time. Her outward distress was nothing compared to what was nagging her on the inside.

It had to be done. She had said her peace. It was going to be done and that was it. Now all she had to do was wait for Abram.

Chapter Eight

DECISIONS, GOSPEL GRACE

GALATIANS 1:10-15

"Am I now seeking the favor of men or of GOD? Or am I trying to please men. If I were still pleasing men, then I should not be a SERVANT of Christ. For the gospel I preach is not a man's gospel...I did not receive it from man, nor was I taught it, but it came through a revelation of Jesus Christ...He who had set me apart before I was born, called me through his GRACE."

Everything I do revolves around the choices I make. Some are obvious and involuntary whereas others are difficult and need careful thought. Even deciding not to do anything is still a choice but indecision isn't the answer if I seek to grow as a Christian.

Verse 10 is a challenge to help me make up my mind about who I serve in this world. It is a difficult choice but one that I must make nonetheless. One of the most challenging things as a Christian is to let go of the world and choose Christ.

People will be quick to ridicule me, judge me and even humiliate me but I can only speak of the things that God has done in MY life and to MY spirit that no other human being has ever managed to do. I cannot use other people's failures and evil behavior as examples or excuses of God's apathy. It isn't selfish either for me to worry about what I need to do to become a better man because the same LOVE that God has shown me is the same LOVE that I must always show to others as well. This is Love without repercussions or strings attached. It's loving others for the sake of it. It sometimes means that people will take advantage of it but what I seek is a clear conscience and I can only ask God for wisdom when I decide to LOVE without expecting anything in return. Galatians 11 also simply draws a line between deciding whether to be on God's side or on the side of men. I cannot have the best of both worlds therefore I have to make a DECISION. I must choose either one or the other. Therefore, that means God wants me to be DECISIVE. Once I make my choice, I can't waver or doubt it. I must stand firm on God's side and trust that everything is in his hands.

Over the course of my life I may have been taught how to do certain things either from my teachers or parents. But what lies in my mind and spirit, whether it's my natural talents or gifts that spark that inspiration that only comes from within is from GOD. Therefore, my DECISIONS can either allow me to have a closer relationship with him or drift further away.

God's ways are higher than any person or thing and that is why he revealed to me the saving Grace of Christ. So, if God provided this revelation, what other great things does he have in store for me if I SEEK HIS FAVOR. God set me apart from everyone else. Verse 15 says that he had a plan for me even before I was born and called ME through his grace. If no one else believes I am special then that is fine because God already thinks that I am. There is a bigger purpose, a special job for me to serve Christ that no other human being can understand and I should never be ashamed about my position. To summarize, this verse encourages me to be DECISIVE with the CHOICES or DECISIONS I make. Once I make the CHOICE to serve CHRIST, He will reveal to me HIS purpose and plan for my life. Finally, I am special in God's eyes. He had a plan for me long before I walked this earth therefore I shouldn't be discouraged even if I don't see the bigger picture.

Chapter Nine

WORKS AND FAITH

Galatians 2:16
"Yet who knows that a man is not justified by WORKS of the LAW but through FAITH in Jesus Christ."

Having a relationship with Christ isn't simply about following a set of rules or checking off a to do list. It's more than just about being rewarded for good behavior. It is an IMMERSIVE experience that is not simply about doing things but also includes what we think as well. In circumstances beyond our control, in situations beyond what we are able to do physically, all God requires of us is to have FAITH. This is because we are all created differently. Not everyone is built like an athlete or has access to resources that help them succeed. Having FAITH appeals not just to the able bodied but to the ones with NOTHING. However dark, bleak or impossible the task is all we must have is FAITH in Christ. It sounds simple and to some people too good to be true. But what is the risk? Whatever you tried before didn't work and you are prone to make the same mistakes over and over again until it's too late. Having FAITH puts you in a position where you have to

42

confront a problem differently. Christ will always give you the help to overcome it.

Chapter Ten

PERSONAL INSTRUCTION

The most important quality I have gained from reading the Bible is taking personal responsibility for my actions. It's something that goes beyond just maturity or experience, but it has taught me to look at myself first and accept my current circumstance (whether good or bad), before blaming others. Like an artist placing a blank piece of paper on a table before they embark on their masterpiece, self-analysis has taught me to start afresh and have a renewed outlook on life. It's allowed me to work with what I have with the hope of improving my situation. I realize now that my mind is my greatest asset and I cannot let it go to waste. These next five verses I've learned simply strengthen my resolve in learning PERSONAL INSTRUCTION

Galatians 5:5 "For through the SPIRIT by FAITH we WAIT for the hope of righteousness."

Bible verses shouldn't be taken literally all the time. Their meaning differs from chapter to chapter and is best understood when taken in the context of what is being talked about. The same principle that applies in understanding the plot of a novel or movie should be taken in discerning the meaning of a verse. For instance, the verse above tells us to WAIT. Waiting requires patience. It requires a calm understanding of when to act and when to let time take its course. God works in a similar way. There are times He requires us to hold back until the moment is right. Therefore, while we wait, God says he has equipped us with two things. The SPIRIT and FAITH. These two are vital because they will guide us in overcoming a specific problem.

God's SPIRIT has different characteristics but for the purpose of this work, I will use the verse within Chapter 5 to illustrate what is within the SPIRIT as we WAIT for God's promise.

Galatians 5:16-17,"WALK by the SPIRIT, and do not GRATIFY the desires of the flesh. For the desires of the flesh are against the SPIRIT and the desires of the spirit are against the flesh."

So we wait through the SPIRIT and how do we wait in the SPIRIT? By walking. Waiting for God's promises doesn't mean we need to be passive. We must WALK by the spirit. Not literally of course but my understanding of this is that No matter how desperate we are there are other areas of our life that need our attention. These verses just illustrate the point that God is still active even when we WAIT on his promise. He is actively working in our favor while we WAIT and, in the meantime, instead of taking too much time worrying, we should simply do what we can in the MOMENT. Verse 17 also points out how separate the spirit is from the body. The Spirit and the flesh are completely opposed to each other. Trusting the SPIRIT is harder sometimes than trusting the BODY because the flesh gives us a present indication of how we feel but doesn't necessarily mean we must immediately act. Doing the right thing means we have to trust in the spirit and not just how we feel.

Galatians 5:5 "For you were called to FREEDOM brethren; only do not use your FREEDOM as an opportunity for the flesh, but through LOVE be SERVANTS of one another."

The FREEDOM that comes with a relationship with Christ isn't a license to do whatever you want with your body but it comes with the RESPONSIBILITY to HELP other people. You shouldn't just use your freedom for your own needs and desires but one of its main purposes is to help others/show love to others when they need it the most. Don't take advantage of the freedom God has given you but value that gift and time and use it to reach out to others.

Galatians 5:25-26 "If we live by the SPIRIT, let us also WALK by the spirit. 26 Let us have no self-conceit, no provoking of one another, no envy of one another."

Walking by the Spirit also means that we shouldn't be too proud of ourselves to think that we are better/superior to other people. Neither should we provoke or encourage them to do wrong. Walking by the Spirit should not make us envious or jealous of other people's accomplishments.

Chapter Eleven

HOW TO RESPOND TO LIFE CHALLENGES

What role does hardship play in my life? The necessity of struggle. How do I respond when I'm faced with a particular problem?

James 1:2-4 "Count it all JOY my brethren when you meet various TRIALS; for you know that the TESTING of your FAITH produces STEADFASTNESS. And let steadfastness have its full effect, that you may be PERFECT and COMPLETE lacking in nothing."

The direct answer to this question is to rely on FAITH. I must first accept that there are things beyond my control and that even though I don't know why they are happening to me or what the outcome is going to be, God PROMISES that in that moment of uncertainty he is with me.

Every time I feel unhappy or face a challenge that's tough to solve, how do I react to it? Do I crumble like a rotting piece of wood? Do I give in to my emotions and let them lead me blindly like a helpless leaf blowing in the wind? Or do I stand firm in the FAITH God gave me, to challenge ANYTHING that comes my way even when I'm afraid. The

48

bible tells me that every test is a challenge to make me rely on God's favor and strength. How I respond to my problems determines whether I'm mature enough to rely on God's strength rather than my own. No matter how difficult the problem is and no matter how much pain I'm in, how I respond to the problem is the first step in solving it. I don't think God expects me to always literally jump up and down with JOY when tragedy strikes but it is a good TEST in determining how well I RESPOND/REACT.

Chapter Twelve

WISDOM

I lack wisdom, I'm not smart enough so WHERE or WHOM can I get WISDOM from? **James 1:5 "If any of you lacks WISDOM let him ASK God, who gives to all men GENEROUSLY and WITHOUT REPROACHING and it WILL be given to him."**

When I'm in a dilemma, who do I turn to for advice? Do I google it on the internet or is there someone I can ask to solve the issue. The bible tells me that I should seek God first not just for advice but for WISDOM. Wisdom I've learned doesn't necessarily mean being top of the class or being the most knowledgeable person on world affairs. Worldly wisdom isn't wrong but it's only a limited explanation of the word. And when I ask God for WISDOM, He listens to me. He doesn't turn away or tell me to come back later. He GENEROUSLY and GENUINELY acts on my very present and immediate need. He knows the importance of having WISDOM and He is willing to give it to me in abundance.

Lord my prayer is that I may have the WISDOM to make the right decisions. I may not be the smartest person in the world or the most eloquent but that won't stop YOU from giving me WISDOM to succeed. God's promises are GUARANTEED only if we put ALL our trust in Him.

CHARACTERISTICS OF WISDOM

What are the characteristics of WISDOM?

Just because I don't have stellar academic credentials that other people have doesn't mean I'm not WISE. There are attributes of WISDOM that no one can teach me but God and this verse explains that point.

"The WISDOM from ABOVE is first PURE, then PEACABLE, GENTLE, OPEN TO REASON, full of MERCY and GOOD FRUITS, without uncertainty or insincerity. And the harvest of the RIGHTEOUS is sown in PEACE by those who make PEACE."

Wisdom is an attribute of my character and not just a sign of how much I know about the world. The wisdom I desire is from God. I must seek it for PURE and not selfish reasons and with the INTENTION to resolve conflict and not start one by aggressively arguing my point.

The wisdom I seek must be FLEXIBLE enough to listen and accept other people's good ideas or opinions and see how it fits into solving a problem. FORGIVING/SHOWING mercy to someone who has wronged me is also another sign of WISDOM and my reward is gaining a friend.

WISDOM means that if I make a decision that is right before God, I shouldn't hesitate to carrying it out. (Be doers and not hearers only deceiving yourselves).

Chapter Thirteen

REWARD FOR ENDURANCE

Do I get rewarded when I respond positively to my trial/problem? YES!

James 1:12 "BLESSED is the man who ENDURES trial, for when he has STOOD the test he will receive the crown of LIFE which God has PROMISED to those who LOVE him"

The things that trouble me the most are the things that God wants to get rid of in my life. It is now my responsibility to actively seek God to COMPLETELY eliminate them. Flirting with sin is flirting with death so even though initially it might seem hard or impossible to achieve, I should EXPECT that something good will come out of ENDURING through my problem no matter how unpleasant it is.

And my reward isn't just based on hope or possibility. God has PROMISED that if I love him, if I am willing to respond POSITIVELY to my problem, he will GUARANTEE and BLESS my reward. Responding positively to a problem is how to put my FAITH into action. I think I'm old enough to know that life isn't all pleasant. It's up to me to decide whether to grudgingly accept this fact and remain pessimistic about everything or foresee and EMBRACE the role that FAITH can play in the challenges in my life so that I can grow and mature.

GIFTS

Where do my GIFTS/TALENTS come from? I think I'm fortunate enough to have certain gifts that most people don't have. I say this with no arrogance whatsoever but with humility that I can do certain things better than the average person. It's probably partly because of the environment I grew up in that allowed me to hone my skills, but mostly because I realized I had an innate PASSION for doing them that no human being could have ever taught or influenced me. And this is where God has played a major part in my development. So why are some people more talented than others? Is it their genes, race or economic background?

For every Ivy League educated millionaire, there is a high school dropout who has been able to beat the odds and make the same millions. Some of the world's best athletes had parents who were not athletic at all in their youth.

James 1:17 "Every GOOD ENDOWMENT and every PERFECT GIFT is from ABOVE, coming down from the father of lights with whom there is no variation or shadow due to change."

I believe that even though God gives us physical gifts that other people can see, admire or compliment us on, the GREATEST gifts are those that he gives us when we believe we lack the physical attributes that make us stand out. These gifts make us stop comparing ourselves to others and accept the uniqueness of how God made us.

In short, it is God who gave me my GIFTS/TALENT and I am thankful to him every day that I have the opportunity to use them. I pray and desire that he may grant me the gifts I lack, not just for my personal pleasure, but to help others as well.

ALL the GOOD THINGS I want/desire/have, are from GOD. Lord give me WISDOM, give me COURAGE, give me DISCIPLINE to make me the LEADER that you want me to be. Amen.

Lord I also know that you do not want me to be content with the gifts I have, but I should also aspire to get gifts that I don't have. This will allow me to do things that I didn't think were even possible for me to do. God will not only use the gifts I possess but create others to make me complete. `

Chapter Fourteen

EMOTIONS AND ANGER
EMOTIONS/How do I deal with ANGER?

When it comes to dealing with my emotions and understanding them, I am very thankful to Joyce Meyer. She often says that our emotions are unreliable, and that we shouldn't make our decisions based on how we feel. Just because I feel angry, sad or indifferent doesn't mean I should immediately act on it. It also doesn't mean that God feels the same way about me. God hasn't stopped loving me, blessing me or protecting me. When I'm offended at someone, the easy thing to do is to get angry at them but the bible tells me that I should be SLOW to ANGER. Anger goes against what God wants to do in my life. Maybe it's a lesson in patience, forgiveness and self-control. Emotions serve their purpose in gauging our response to things but I shouldn't solely rely on them to make ALL my decisions.

"Let every man be QUICK to HEAR slow to speak and slow to ANGER, for the anger of man does not work the RIGHTEOUSNESS of God."

Chapter Fifteen

THE WORD/ Acting on the WORD

I remember the desperation, anxiety and helplessness I felt after I graduated from college. I lacked any sense of purpose or direction in my life. Emotionally, at the time I had nowhere to turn to and felt like a wreck. I was at a personal crisis. Nowhere to live, no job, no future to look forward to and I felt my degree hadn't prepared me for real life. That's when I made up my mind to ask God for help with my LIFE. It was at this point I decided to finally ACT on the word of God. To this day, it's been the best DECISION I've ever made despite all the new challenges that have come my way since then. Right before I made the decision I remember saying to myself that If God was who He claimed to be, I needed his help to heal my broken spirit.

He duly answered my plea and instantly filled my heart with joy in a way that no person on this earth would ever give me. The greatest irony was that even though that was my lowest point in life, I'd never felt happier in that moment. I thank my mom for being the perfect example of how to live a Christ-like life and if I can only become half the person she is, I think I'll be ok. My Bible became my best friend and God was my confidant. ACTING on the WORD means DOING what God requires me to do without question. All my relationships, sports, education failed to fill the void in my heart and my desperate craving for attention, love and recognition was not only insatiable but selfish. They say desperate times call for desperate measures and God IS and will ALWAYS be my source of HOPE.

What good will it do me, talking about how God changed my life if I can't practice what I preach? Hypocrisy will lead to my downfall because I'm not just fooling/DECEIVING myself but God. **"But be DOERS of the WORD and not hearers only deceiving yourselves."** Put my money where my mouth is!!!!!!!!!!! I must put my faith into action because if I don't, I'm lying to myself.

Chapter Sixteen

RELIGION; what is it?

James 1:27 says that, "RELIGION that is PURE and UNDEFILED before God and the father is this: to VISIT orphans and widows in their affliction, and to keep oneself unstained from the world."

Isn't religion what Christ fought against? It divides us and pits one side against the other. But if we do consider ourselves to be religious, we should go out of our way/get out of our comfort zone to help those in need. How do I comfort a child who has lost both parents and is forced to go into foster care because they have no other relatives to take care of them? How do I tell a child who was abandoned by his mother and left to fend for himself that God loves him?

How do I comfort a single mother of five whose husband died in a car crash and was the sole breadwinner of the family? These are some of the real life situations people face and it is my DUTY if I go the "religious route" to ACTIVELY HELP/VISIT those who are less fortunate than I am. If I claim to be without sin, what am I doing to help others? Is my PURITY simply there to show how different I am from everyone else?

No. Purity will require doing things I wouldn't normally feel comfortable doing but doing them because of a higher (not personal) purpose.

Chapter Seventeen

HOW SHOULD I TREAT OTHERS? RESPECT/ WE ARE ALL THE SAME

When I lived in Bowling Green, I was fortunate to have friends from literally all over the world. Argentina, México, England, Jamaica Zambia, Bulgaria, Russia and Ethiopia were just some of the places. We never really had deep conversations about culture or politics but all I remember is that they respected me, and I respected them.

I've played on teams where no one hardly spoke any English, but it's never bothered me. Regardless of the language or religious barrier, as a Christian, I'm expected to RESPECT others. On a basic level, the same God who made me is the same God who made them.

"Show NO PARTIALITY as you HOLD the FAITH of our Lord Jesus Christ, the Lord of GLORY."

This verse is ultimately about RESPECT. I might disagree with others on different issues, but I must explain my POSITION clearly and with DIGNITY. Class is permanent. Unless the person decides to put hands on me then......!!!!I kid I kid.

Chapter Eighteen

PUTTING FAITH INTO ACTION: How can I put my FAITH TO WORK?

For the bigger issues in my life I've learnt that I must have FAITH. I want to have a FAMILY one day, a secure job to help me take care of my needs. And I'm confident that God will provide these things for me when it's the right time.

I must apply my FAITH to my day to day activities. How do I treat others? Am I spending my time wisely by getting closer to God, or wasting my time watching TV and movies? What decisions am I actively making to prepare myself for what God has for me in the future? I can't claim to have FAITH in God and do what I want. When I'm not sure what I need to do, it's the perfect opportunity to PRAY to God and ask Him about it.

James 2:17 "So FAITH by itself, if it has no WORKS is DEAD."

Chapter Nineteen

SPEECH, TONGUE AND WHAT I SAY
TEAM NO FILTER!

We all know that one person who says WHATEVER they want to say regardless of the setting, occasion, or company they keep. They blurt out the first thing that pops into their head. Whether what they say is meant as scathing criticism or as a joke, people react to the comment uncomfortably either by averting their eyes away from the person or by trying to change the topic to avoid the embarrassment of making things worse. But no. Human beings of this kind do not conform to the hideous rules of respect or etiquette like you and I do. They are not bound by the chains of self-control. They are rebels who are forever loyal in their ability to create shock awe by the words they spew.

Instead of getting the hint, they relish the opportunity to make people squirm in their seats and go on and on, hoping to win someone over with their foul-mouthed rant and ill-timed humor. You either love them for their brazen attempts to stand out from the crowd or hate them eternally for just not keeping their mouths shut. But in hindsight I'm no different. I have said things I shouldn't have said. It's like the mouth has a mind of its own sometimes but I'm thankful that I have enough self-control not to talk about certain issues at certain times. So when you say something you aren't supposed to say or know someone who has no filter, remember this verse.

James 3:8-10 "(But) no human being can TAME the TONGUE- a restless evil full of deadly poison. With it we bless the Lord and father, and with it we curse men, who are made in the likeness of God. From the same MOUTH come BLESSING and CURSING." It's like the mouth was made just to say something stupid and this verse is my reminder that if I have nothing good to say, I shouldn't say it at all.

Chapter Twenty

MY RELATIONSHIP WITH THE WORLD AND GOD.

How does my relationship with THE WORLD affect my relationship with God? I know the things that prevent me from getting closer to God. Sometimes the more I try to stay away from them, the harder they come back. I feel trapped, lonely and miserable. Every relationship I've been in so far always seems to end in bitter disappointment. I'm convinced I have my priorities all messed up so I have to change the way I see and do things. If the things I pursued in the past didn't make me happy, then what's the point of following the same isolated path? My lifestyle has to drastically change so that I can be what God wants me to be. I'm far from perfect but I cannot afford to make the same mistakes I made in college, especially when it comes to relationships.

I had a habit of settling for less and for the wrong reasons and only got what I deserved when things went bad. I have to break away from the past and stop wishing that things could have ended up differently. I can't force someone to like me so I have to forget about them just to maintain my own sanity. God knows my thoughts and the desires of my heart that's why I feel it's pointless to write down specifics. What's done is done. If I'm distracted by the WORLD, I'll never get closer to God. My first priority is God and he will help me navigate through life. **"Do you not know that friendship with the WORLD is enmity with GOD? Therefore, whoever wishes to be a friend of the world makes himself an enemy of God."** I need to respect women for the right reasons. That way genuine friendships develop that will hopefully lead to relationships.

In your time Lord, in your perfect time. But first teach me how to become a man.

Chapter Twenty-One

HUMILITY

Stay Humble. You are not as big as you think you are.

I don't like talking about myself. Sometimes because I honestly don't have anything interesting to say but mostly because I'd rather not talk about my life. I have bad memories from the past that I want to keep between me and God. I opened up once to someone I thought I loved but no good came out of it. Wait! Wait! Now I just sound bitter. Blaming others for the mistakes I made. I'm thankful that God is in my life because without him I would have given up years ago. The job I have now came at the right time and physically I feel better than I've ever felt. I still have a lot to accomplish but thank you for being there for me Lord when I needed you the most. "HUMBLE yourself before the Lord and he will EXALT you."

Chapter Twenty-Two

THE FUTURE AND TOMORROW

The future

I want to act like I know what's going to happen tomorrow. I want to believe that I am in control of my life and my destiny. I want to make predictions, claims, assumptions and theories based on what I want my future to be. What I want and what God wants for me are very different. I want the beautiful wife, the nice car and the big house in the suburbs. There's nothing wrong with that. What troubles me are my thoughts, my intentions. Is my life made once I achieve all these things I dream of? Is my FUTURE finally secure? Sometimes I compare the good things that God has done in my life in the present and compare them to how I felt without them in the past. I came to a damning conclusion.

I wasted a lot of valuable time and energy WORRYING about the FUTURE which God had clearly provided and taken care of.

My LIFE isn't my own. It is God's. Therefore, this verse is a reminder that I must acknowledge my future plans, projects, hopes and dreams to the FATHER who takes care of all my needs. I should constantly ask myself this question when I feel worried and uncertain about my future. What can I do NOW to please God?

"You do not know about TOMORROW? What is your LIFE? For you are a mist that appears for a little time and then vanishes. Instead you ought to say, "If the Lord WILLS, we shall live, and we shall do this or that."

My life is in God's hands therefore I should be very careful about what I do and say. This verse answers these questions. What will happen to my life in the future? I don't know.

But what is certain is that if I align my life with God's teaching, He PROMISES that He will take care of me regardless of what happens.

What IS my life? The Bible says that my LIFE is like a mist and before I know it, I could be gone. As brief and as abrupt as my life is, don't I have a purpose? Yes, but it is God who will give me that purpose if I put my trust/my life in Him.

Reference this to the verse in Matthew about the future.

Chapter Twenty-Three

PRAYER

Does God answer PRAYER?

Yes. When I prayed to God that He would heal me from my sickness, He did. When I prayed to God that He would keep me in school when I was about to get kicked out, He listened to me and answered my prayer. When I prayed to God that He would help me graduate after I believed that I had blown my chance, He made it possible. I prayed for a job and He gave it to me even when I didn't deserve it. I cannot speak for other people and answer for the choices they make. I can only speak for myself and share the wonderful and complex ways in which God works. I refuse to believe that things just happen. There has to be more to life than just all these things around me. My random existence among billions of people across the globe isn't just a coincidence. I have a PURPOSE and that purpose is to please God despite all my imperfections and insecurities.

I wish I got everything I prayed for as quickly as I write down these words, but to appreciate pleasure I have to endure pain. The only certainty is that God is ALWAYS with me. God sees my good deeds; He listens to my prayers and wants to reward me.

"The PRAYER of a RIGHTEOUS man has great POWER in its effects."

FINAL THOUGHTS

When it comes to Christ, NEVER compromise. Never settle for anything less just because you FEEL like it. The Holy Spirit is the voice of reason when you're doubtful, afraid or uncertain about the future. Learn to experience God's love for yourself rather than what you hear from other people. Pick up the Bible and study the word of God diligently.

All about the Author

Stephen Ochieng is a teacher, writer, editor, and a graduate of Journalism from Bowling Green State University, Ohio. If not for Christ, his trials and tribulations would be dictated by Chelsea Football Club and The Chicago Bulls.

www.ingramcontent.com/pod-product-compliance
Lightning Source LLC
Chambersburg PA
CBHW060701030426
42337CB00017B/2706